I0170487

# Liminal

## The Spaces Between

Elizabeth Carson

Copyright © 2025 Elizabeth Carson
All rights reserved.
ISBN: 978-1-7380938-6-1 (paperback)

978-1-7380938-7-8 (ebook)


Cover art and design: Elizabeth Carson

# Dedication

This collection is for all the nameless people who have created magic in our world; who have spun ideas and imaginings, thoughts to challenge and delight; who have known despair and come out the other side with something new to offer.

In short, for just about everyone. Because life itself is magic, is mysterious, is liminal.

# Table of Contents

# Liminal

## The Spaces Between

# About Words

Words, being concrete, limit interpretation,
transform transitional into tangible
and block the flow,
the tossing-in-the-wind flow,
of imagination.

They can't help it.
As symbols of what now exists,
they cut off access
to invisible, inexpressible, half-perceived
realities.

That's the challenge:
to break the walls, to modulate words
into unfoldings,
defying barriers.

Daunting, really, to put aside the book,
full as it is of words, and wander
(or wonder)
in places ill defined,
not seen
by any but you.

# Hope and Gold

Gold: immutable yet malleable.
Store it as bars in vaults, pound it to translucency,
wear it as a commitment,
but remember, it keeps to itself,
avoids alliances.

Does this make it a proper container for hope?

Hope: infinitely malleable, easily mutable,
adjusting to the situation,
to the mood of the times, the mood of the person.
Hope, they say, springs eternal, but that's a lie.
Unless nurtured, hope can die
as readily as anything organic dies.

Where, then, to store hope,
to nurture it into long life?
In gold?

The sunrise blazed golden today
because of smoke from forest fires,
not for any hopeful reason:
tragedy mutated into glory.

Into promise, into heart-lifting – dare I say it? – hope.

Golden hope, in the face of conflagration.
Golden hope, buffed to high shine,
what is left
when all else is lost.

# Autumn Morning

Dawn doesn't so much break as seep
through layers of fog,
lit from within, opalescent.

The sharp-edged land lies unknowable,
the horizon a thing of imaginings.

Inevitably, the sun does its work,
and the fog succumbs, now mere wisps,
lingering reminders of something undefined.
They hover over valleys, cutting through trees and hills
before themselves evaporating.

The day greets the earth,
all is made plain.

Accountants and lexicographers will be happy.
Dreamers, less so.

# Dementia

I don't know, but I suspect
that dementia is a liminal space,

An uncertain drifting, nebulous doors
that open to doubt, or to nothing at all.

A space in which simple tasks
    (and by whose authority dare I define
    a task as simple?)
become incomprehensible.

A space in which thoughts drift, untamed and lost,
and words lose meaning far too soon.

# On a Sunday Morning

Sunday morning, I check the time,
I glance at my watch,
    (does anyone look to watches anymore?)
and there's only one hand, the long one
    (discounting that freaky second hand
    chugging along).

Only one hand. What??

Clearly, time has stopped. No more hours.
In a silent Sunday morning house
it's easy enough to believe.

Alternate Universe Time!

Tell it to the cats, asleep by the hearth,
ignoring this perturbation in the universe.

Tell it to a logical mind, the one that's tired of logic,
the one that thinks
it would be kind of cool
if physics went haywire.

Ah, well. The minute hand shifts,
revealing the missing hour underneath.
Just as well, but still...

The cats perk up,
consulting some inner clock.
It must be time for lunch.

# Haiku I

Fifty metre pool
behind me, my workout done,
hot shower awaits.


The softness of things:
adagio, piano,
cat's ear, a hand's touch.


Sounds within a storm:
rush of wind tearing at trees,
drums on the skylight.


Air brushes my face,
sweet scent borne on gentle breeze,
arrival of spring.


Your hand to steady
my monster-slaying rapier:
facing the demons.


Look out! Here they come!
Daydreams lure me far away
from the here and now.

# Leaving Behind

A friend retired
and put away her wristwatch.
She's rarely what I might call 'on time',
and if, as she believes, this drives me crazy,
well, she also surely knows
that's my issue, not hers.

Time has been monetized,
each minute, hour, month
of value to someone,
and rewarded.

Payday.

Leaving behind the watch
is payback, reward
for time spent, for timecards punched.
My friend has developed her own rhythm,
a so-called 'time' that has little to do
with cultural expectation or financial necessity.
She accomplishes when and as she will
and is happy.

The fetter of the watch
is well cast aside.

(And no, I don't really mind.)

# Neither Here nor There

The strip between land and sea,
both one and the other,
defines neither.
Ephemeral, ever changing,
this is a liminal place
where magic is not merely possible,
it is mandated, inevitable.

You could say the land dominates,
with its stern solidity,
but look. The sea shapes, patterns,
occasionally obliterates.

Its strength is fluid, its whisper a warning:
I can sweep you away, beware.

Walking on the wet sand,
I take the risk, defy that voice,
feel the solid grit underfoot,
the tug as the ocean rushes in, out.

For a brief time, I too am nowhere,
undefined by land or sea,
immovable, flowing.

# Cookie

Coffee morning. We sit together chatting,
as one does,
and a plate of cookies is passed around.
Three women, three cookies.

Filled cookies, these, an old tradition,
white fondant between layers of chocolate biscuit.

Motion becomes synchronized, almost balletic:
Each holds her cookie horizontal,
and with her free hand
twists the top layer.

(By now, I bet you know what kind of cookie it is.)

All eat the naked top layer
amid discussion about the intricacy of the pattern
incised on the outside, surely unchanged for...
how many years?

Ah, but there's room for variation.
One peels off the oh-so-sweet icing
for solo consumption.
The others opt for melded textures,
the chocolate, the... call it the flavor of white.

Even the oldest of us, ninety now,
grew up with these cookies.
We all remember the correct way
		– the *only* way –
to eat them.

# New Yesterdays

So, about yesterday. Gone, but where?

Missing in action – we can't go back, they say,
because yesterday's reality is pliable,
shaped by the brain's quirks
into a semi-truth that suits today.

Minds adapt, memories transform,
and there are no hard past tenses.

# Terra Sees to Business

I watch. Terra hovers, unmoving,
her eyes far-seeing, focused on nothing,
her face intense.

Ah, what concentration! What depth!

Until, her purpose achieved,
she becomes all business,
scratching in the litter box,
tossing little grains about.

Pooping, it turns out, is a soulful business.

She goes on her way,
assuming, correctly,
that further cleanup isn't her job.

# Remarks

Open up a remark,
study its innards.

(By which I mean,
divine its true intent.)

Remarks are casual things,
skilled at slipping in
where they may not be welcome.

Tossed off carelessly
(or not),
not meant to change the trajectory.

But they do.

Because remarks have sticky glue
all over them.

They ride home with the listener,
(or sometimes with the utterer,
who may be rethinking).

They hang around, growing in power.

Tricky things, remarks.
Their danger teaches
tongue-biting has its merits.

# Lest

Lest – a gateway word
defending us against what is not
and – some would argue – should not be.

A word calling for the subjunctive
to, you know, heighten the mystery.

A word implying diminution, a lesser-ness,
saying, if you buy into what comes after,
you lose.

Lest you think this be idle rambling,
allow me to remind you
of all the things you were warned against,
and did anyway.

Bad news, eh?

Or wait. Did you take a warning-against
and turn it on its head?

The failure of lest: not all gates are barriers.
Some are waiting, positively begging
for you to break them down.

Take that road, take it today,
lest you miss the experience of a lifetime.

## That First Connection

Nothingness evaporates,
this-moment reality smacks us in the face,
drawing us to a place exclusively ours,
     (if we dare)
present only in shared surrender.

A longing unfolds, leading me
     (or you, or us)
into enchantment, a liminal world
of not quite, but maybe.

# Paint by Numbers

The leaves form a paint-by-number pastiche,
autumn colors so expected, so vivid
    as to be trite
were they not beyond glory.

But the picture holds anomalies....

This year, it's the end of November,
and half the trees still flaunt green,
half the shrubs are in bud.

Well, it was predicted,
has been predicted for years.

There is no wisdom in the lingering green,
the out-of-season blooming in the garden.
This is wrong, and we know it.

This is the verdict, the final warning.
We have destroyed the balance, killed it,
hidden the corpse
behind blazing fall colors.

# Too Much

Stuff bookends my life
and weighs it down.

Stuff.

Despite periodic culls,
it abounds, it proliferates,
it surrounds me.

Do I need
    – shelves of books I'll never read again
     (or possibly never read at all),
    – four ukuleles,
    – six frying pans?

Stuff.

My clothes closet bulges,
despite the boring fact
that I live in flannel work shirts,
while the rest just hang there.

Do these garments give me joy?
Could I part with some of my dozens of scarves
(which I haven't worn since pre-hot-flash days,
    to be honest)?
Or my handkerchief collection?
How often do I consult my books
on watercolor painting? On cooking?

Am I brave enough
to enact a good winnowing,
lighten the load?

Or will my poor heirs end up with
beads and fabric and yarn,
unworn clothes and underused kitchen appliances
from long-forgotten projects?

Probably. Poor heirs.
But they will suffer fewer qualms
when my things go off to charity.

They will be able to do what I can't...
not quite yet.

# Long Gone

Tumbling backwards down a rabbit hole...

Once, there were department stores,
   remember?

My mom took me downtown; I wore a hat,
and we lunched – *Lunched! Best Behavior!* –
in a department store restaurant.

Later, I could go with a friend on the bus.
I still have a mouse pin I bought,
a couple of escalator rides up,
more than half a century ago.

And oh, those Christmas window displays!

Once, we had a place to buy our undies,
our silver polish,
our raincoats, our vacuum cleaners.
To browse the departments,
to dream.

Is anything left that isn't online?

A book-length elegy could be written to
these bastions of domestic commerce.

I don't really need anything.
But I miss the event, the experience,
secure in the (misplaced) confidence
the department store would always be there.

# A Delight of Crows

Several dozen crows stopped by tonight,
with raucous commentary.

They have their designated routes,
arrive according to a system
not understood by me,
but staking their claim nonetheless
to trees and rooftops and roadways.

They strut their pride, an exuberant invasion.
Loudly, they caw their existence.
I wouldn't dare disapprove.

# A Hymn of Thanks to Whatever Powers May Be

Thank you for my health,
and should my health give way,
thank you for supporting me
as I accept enforced down time
and honor my body in its challenges.

Thank you for my family,
and when they pee outside the litter box,
thank you for the patience
to respect their limitations
and love them anyway.

Thank you for my friends,
and when they hurt, or desert,
thank you for the tests
of clear hearing, fair response,
and acceptance.

Thank you for financial security
and when the budget gets tight,
thank you for resourcefulness
and for showing me
how little is really needed.

Thank you for my home,
and should disaster strike,
by earthquake, fire,
or any imagined horror,
thank you for resilience, and acceptance,
and courage.

Thank you for the beauties of the world,
and when I fail to see the beauty,
thank you for putting it out there anyway,
until I wake up.

Thank you for the power to create,
a friendship, a spreadsheet, a loaf of bread.
Help me always to be awake
to the possibility
of adding goodness to the world.

Thank you for the cycle of birth, death, and beyond.
Help me to accept my finitude,
and live fully, without fear
of the grand transition ahead.

Thank you for the everyday things,
the vegetable peeler that peels,
the phone to keep me in touch,
the hot water that flows from the shower.
And when the peeler won't peel,
the phone needs charging,
and the water runs cold,
Thank you for reminding me
that it really doesn't matter.

Thank you for my times of deep communion,
and when my mind jabbers ceaselessly,
the inspiration won't come,
and the world seems soulless,
Thank you for being the guiding hand on my shoulder
until I find my way again.

## Assassination

Here is what I don't understand:
How can what I am,
what I look like, what I think,
the ordinary things I do,
make you want to kill me?

The sights, smells, tastes of the earth
are no one's to deny to another,
are a gift given.

For any person to say
these things may no longer be yours...
Worse than sacrilege,
this is desecration.

# Old Age

It's a liminal time, and those who are clever
don't dwell too much on it;
dwelling *in* it is quite enough.

The entrance is clear enough, although the borders may
fluctuate,
  the dreams of youth and middle age, left behind,
  long-ago loves and abandoned dreams, gone.

What's left is the uncertainty of now.

The exit is clear, although the timing is elusive,
as is the circumstance.

It's as if life has lost itself
and new definitions are needed.

In this hallowed, haunted time,
the only option is to forge forward,
cheerfully aware,
defying the odds, defying desolation,
defying the mysterious future place
that ultimately will claim you.

# Arcs

I have been contemplating the arcs of life, building on
something I heard on the radio, half listening
over my morning bagel and to-do lists.

Birth to old age is an arc...
but may be incomplete
should old age not be attained –
a rainbow half formed.
> (And an aside: haven't I promised myself
> never, *never*,
> to compose a poem involving rainbows?)

Then there's innocence to experience.
Surely, though, there's no continuum,
one to the other,
much less a guarantee.
So, another incomplete arc.

Well, then, from ignorance to educated.
If we're talking just the facts, ma'am, this might qualify,
from the simplest survival techniques
to the art of the handshake,
understanding string theory, winning the lass,
or even parsing a sentence
> (and show me anyone under, say, fifty,
> who can do this).

And would you care to speculate (perhaps not)
on the educated, profoundly ignorant adults you've met?

Okay, this is going nowhere.

So imagine this: no arc. Instead, an enormity, a space

waiting to be filled with echoes
of beauty and discovery,
a view so vast it defies comprehension.
Now launch yourself
into that chaotic, ripe space,
give yourself over to its vastness,
unformed, unshaped, no trajectory,
and there you are,
no arcs, just you.

Just You.

# A Key

Today's key unlocks Handel.
It's a fingering chart for a descant recorder.
Master the key, and I'll play
a never-heard-before (by me) sonata.

There are other keys,
lots of them.
A book on origami, key to multitudes
        of peace cranes.

Cat treats, key to wooing a stubborn feline,
tricking her into compliance.
Worth a try, anyway.

A recipe, key to gastronomic exploration;
the sun, to lure me outdoors;
a book, unlocking worlds unexplored.

That key in your hand; haven't you used it
        a dozen times, a million?
Here's a thought:
try, instead, a new one,
all polished and shiny.

Be ready, though.
On the other side of its door...
Amazements.

# Reality in the Morning

How to bear it all?
Easiest to not think, or not know?

It's about the newspaper this morning.

Fires everywhere, but also floods
        defying human supremacy.
Summits for peace failing,
Plastics convention failing,
Relief for Gaza, failing.

The global economy under threat,
my country under threat.

Life as we know it,
under threat.

You get used to it,
but you can't not know.

Perhaps it's just the dark, gray morning,
rare in the summer where I live.

But wait. With the rain,
the garden's been washed and polished,
a sparkling tribute to all that's good and holy.

How can it possibly be all so impossible?

# Past Truths

What a strange thing is history.

At most, clues tell you what went before.
Pottery shards, monuments, buildings, the written word
are only a part of it, and not
the nitty gritty.

Find, one day, an abandoned house in a wood.
Once-loved wallpaper clings imperfectly to walls,
an organ with rotted bellows, left behind in the parlor.
      (Why?)
The outline of an overgrown garden that fed a family,
a volunteer cabbage marking the place,
waiting.

But they are gone, the long-ago occupiers
of this isolated home.
Imprints of ghosts offer up suggestions only, whispering
remember... does anyone, anywhere, remember?

# Sleep

Sleep is the negation of words,
the denial of hard-edged logic.

Sleep is shelter from so-called reality,
when phantasmic uncertainty
comes out to play.

Sleep is refuge,
a chance to put away facts
and romp for a while with God.

# Shadows

Shadows gather and dance
at the foot of the stairs.
I should turn on the light
(better than risking a fall)
but I know these stairs well
and the shadows can't intimidate me.

It's one a.m.,
the dark time.
I do not want the light,
not now.

On my way to the kitchen for a cocoa,
I choose to dissolve into the shadows,
allow them to make up a mystery
so often hidden behind blaring day.

# Haiku II

Wake the haunted mind,
play the viol clear and low
through the green-tinged glade.

In the silence, cats,
a single, plaintive Miaow,
echoing my own.

A line of ducklings
scudding through bog-black waters, hide
within the cattails.

Interlocking cells,
dandelion seed head, gone
in a puff of breath.

Roses, a dahlia,
baby's breath, dried by nature:
Happy Mother's Day.

Airplane propeller,
elegant, the air controlled
by a manmade god.

My recycling bin,
detritus from a week's life,
won't solve anything.

# Mull

Mull belongs to mortars and pestles
grinding away, aroma of bruised spices
filling the senses.

Mulled wine, mulled cider,
the depths of winter, a warming fire.
Or celebrating autumn, when reds and golds
invoke the flavor of allspice.

Grind cold, troublesome thoughts together,
transmogrify them into something warmer, tastier,
sweet and spicy and oh, so tempting.
Then add those thoughts to your drink, to your baking,
to whatever needs a little warmth.

Feels good? Is it promise or memory?
Is this a place you long to go? A place you have been?

A place to reclaim?
Mull it over.

# Giveth

The Lord giveth, and boy
does he give big.
But then the Lord taketh away.

Arguably, this great gift of All That Is
is now.

I would like to believe it isn't temporary.
I'd like to believe there's more.
Conservation of Energy, that reliable law,
says nothing is ever lost.
Does that include thoughts?
Imagination?
Learning?

Can Physics predicate an afterlife?

We've expended plenty
creating after-lives,
the promise of glory, or punishment,
depending.

We're part of the performance here,
kicking the sawdust,
dancing in the circus tent like clowns,
troubling, to no good purpose,
about the exit.

# Hate

Hate is a hard-edged word,
worthy of being spat out like gristle.
A word to trigger the gag reflex,
a word best unspoken,
as if freeing it into the open air,
far from purifying,
pollutes what had been clear.

Hate – a word
that carries acrid burdens.
But then, I speak from my own perspective,
rose tinted, lacking comprehension
for those in its grasp.

Today, I looked out
at blooming cherries,
as, pursuing my thoughts on hate,
I spoke the word
and watched it dissipate, lose its edge,
grow soft and airy as a cherry blossom.

Why can't it be that easy?

Dear Merciful Heavens, I'd like to believe.
I'd like the spring air to be the stronger force,
cleansing life of darkness
and the drab, life-denying canker
of hate.

# Sapphire

She sliced into our lives, hard facets of sapphire,
a crystalline blue freezing the houses, the gardens,
turning reds to purples, whites to aquamarine,
obliterating the rusts of autumn.
This is no modest arrival.

Throughout the winter she blocked corners,
froze thoroughfares to a standstill,
painted pond surfaces
        achingly icy blue,

Nothing stopped her; nothing held her back.

Nothing, that is, until
a crocus defied the sapphire –
a yellow one, as it happens.

She went her way then, with one last
hard crystal edge,
one final pass
before vanishing in an indigo sky.

# Surcease

It's an invasion, the state of things,
the weight of it all bowing your back,
blurring your vision,
isolating you in hollows.

Me, I take myself to the garden,
spend an hour weeding and admiring.

It helps.

# The Naming of Cats

Eliot said
that only a cat
knows her true name.

Eliot was right, of course.
Our cats accept their human-bestowed monikers
    pragmatically,
but could just as well do without.

Dogs are different,
happy enough with Rover or Lassie or whatever.
The dog-human bond is like that,
slavish, lacking due consideration
of the rightness, or not, of the name.

But a cat...
oh, she's happy
to cleave (with claws) to any proof of superiority,
not that she needs further evidence.

She's well aware of who the true mistress is.
That name is merely
something to signal food time,
something to lull a girl to sleep
under lazy strokes and cooing words
when nothing more interesting intrudes.

# Melancholy

Melancholy hangs transparent in the air today.
It's a soft touch of blues, and I find
I don't much mind it.
I'm okay with setting aside ebullience for longing.

Less subtle feelings will return tomorrow,
no doubt.

I'll take melancholy today.
In it lives the fodder for dreams,
far away and subtle,
satisfying in their gauze-like unreality,
but ripe, if I choose, for exploration.

Melancholy adds a tinge of shadow
to the palette of my life,
clarifies, reminds me of
the depths of living.

# The End of the Known World

It's all coming crashing down,
and I don't know how to navigate this,
I don't even know
    what to wish for.

It's not sustainable, what we have now.
Furthermore, it's just wrong.

But what's better?
And what's the cost?

Of course I mean the cost to me.
I'm comfortable, I can live
just how I choose to
without worry.

Most can't.

And I shouldn't.

Prediction: the future won't be pretty.

Perhaps doom is the best option
in a world without the will to change.

# Up-Rising

Bubbles replace balloons
as being more environmentally responsible.
They float up, up,
toward a god
who may or may not pay attention...
who may or may not be there at all.

Plants crack the pavement,
marks on the doorframe track the children's progress,
reaching, always up,
until finally, like Jack's beanstalk,
like those bubbles,
they transcend the blue
and achieve the unknown.

Up defies us to remain
down below.
And when we get up there?
When there is no more up to surpass?
Back to level ground. Flat earth
(we learn, with a landing thump)
has a lot to recommend it.

# Weeds

Wander bemused
in a seed head of salsify
for even a minute,
and know.

Here lies magic.

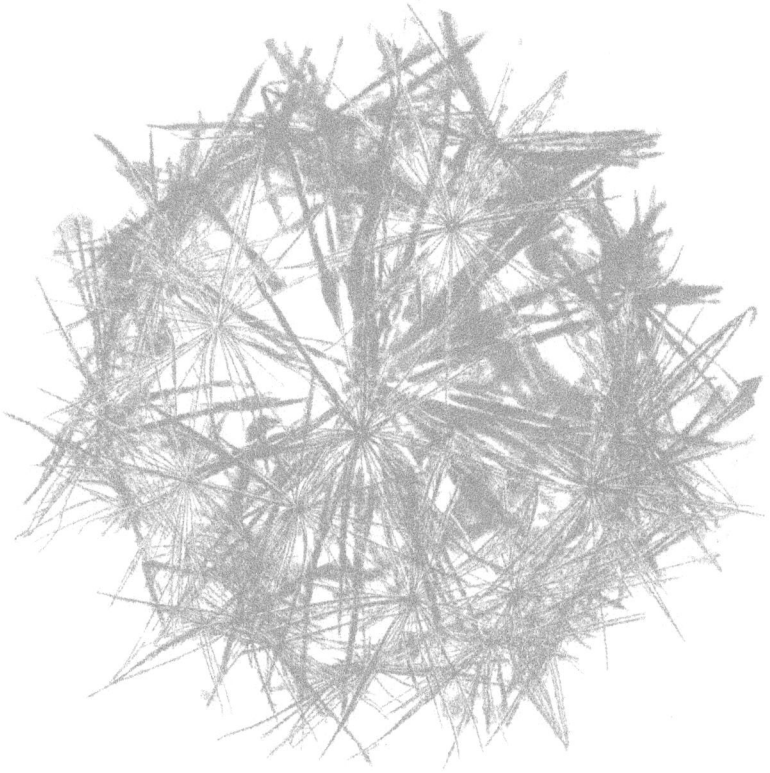

# Reflection on the General Confession

Words lofty, not mundane,
yet by what right dare they
seduce me, reduce me
into naming myself unworthy?

# Silver Trails

Rain, after a golden summer,
creates lines crossing the glass
against a charcoal sky.

The old longing returns.

Do I pine for a past that wasn't,
something other, undefinable
but feeling very real?

Now, though, there's a new twist. Now it's about
time passing too quickly,
and fear, that it all ends so soon,
times and places never, now, to be mine.

Oh, it hurts.
And forget sweet melancholy.
This is sharper, bites deeper.

Turnings and changes…
the tracks on the pane cross, merge.
The story's not over yet, and perhaps it's as well
I'll never know the ending.

# Waiting for Treatment

It's the endlessness, the delays,
one test leading to another,
interminably,
too much time between,
too much time to fear the end result.

(It feels like a television series, manufactured crises,
never-ending dramas...
only it's real.)

An outcome defines a boundary,
one to be crossed, or crashed into.
Dreading the final appointment:
do I want to know?

Yes, after this time
from within my wobbly walls,
I think I do.

# Lonely People

Lonely people gaze from windows
as life goes about its business,
    indifferent.

Wonder how, wonder why.

Lonely people
dream of others, out there,
with someones to meet, places to be.

Lonely people conjure different lives,
strangers to the gnawing need.

Lonely people imagine
they are the only ones.

# Washing Hands

Pouring from one hand to the other,
suds, water, spectres, beginnings and endings,
knowing that I know, at once,
    nothing
      and all I ever shall.

# Hobbled

It could be worse. I could have gout.

The other day, I made the mistake
of venturing out on a decent-length walk
in a pair of untested shoes.

The next day... oh my Goddess! Cramps!
Shin splints! Pain! Not Good!

So, I'm condemned to days of lazing about the house,
hobbling, tentative stretching,
while the sun does all it can
to lure me out.

The whole thing appeals to my essential laziness,
but, considering all sides fairly,
I am a woman who walks.

Ah, well. This morning
things are much better.
I could venture out later, but on the other hand...

Yes. Rain.
Maybe tomorrow.

# Snow in Westmount

Where it began: A graystone house
with servant's quarters tucked in the back,
    behind the galley kitchen,
and a tiny walled garden hosting a scavenging squirrel.
The bachelors living in the house when I knew it
    had no servants.
Private bedroom each, with shared bath.
    (Except the lucky guy who got the servant's quarters:
    he had his own.)
Its past uses, the lives of some family
able to afford a row house in lower Westmount,
cast no reflection on its contemporary inhabitants.

And it snowed.

Montreal, 1968, and from the house on Elm Street
it was a walk in the snow to Westmount Square
    with its grocery and glitz.
the Forum, the Metro, a fondue restaurant close by.
The bow-windowed living room featured an arch
into a dining room fit for banquets.
The furniture must have come with the house,
formal, old.

And still it snowed,
culture shock for a girl from Atlanta.

Snow frames the memory,
because snow shaped my first year in Montreal:
    salt and slush unkind to boots,
    slippery sidewalks, wind fierce enough
    to skid you onto Dorchester Street,
and I dared not drive on snow-painted roads.

It's still there, the house on Elm Street.
It looks good, fifty years on.
Other inhabitants build memories now,
so many different lives,
and the house keeps its secrets.

# Haunting

You turn up when I least expect it:
a parking lot in the rain,
a protest crowd on the news,
in evening shadows,
I see you, or sense you, when I don't want to,
and it's not fair.

I don't choose to be haunted.
I release you, I let you go
to whatever comes next.

In this life, I'm ready
to be left alone.

# Late Season Snowstorm

One boot ahead of the other,
scrunch, scrunch,
and here comes a hill.

Moving forward, left right left.
Graceful post-snowfall dunes
shrink with the warming day.

The decaying snow reveals history,
hollows of human steps,
small ovals – deer perhaps?
Tiny scratches of foraging birds.
All of life has been here, it seems,
trekking through the snow.

One boot, the other boot, up a hill, down.
Dig in a heel, a toe,
secure a foothold
trust there's no black ice underneath.

A hint of grass shows
along the edge of the path,
the green stark in contrast – in expectation.
There a tire track, here a heather poking through,
defiantly purple.

And wouldn't you know, it's raining,
the reason every self-respecting coat
has a hood.
Should have brought an umbrella...

# Facing the Future

Friends say, would you even want to survive?

How on earth to answer that? How to know?
To readily forsake the wonder that is life
without putting up a good fight feels, well, just wrong.

But there may be truth there, should life become,
as they say,
nasty and brutish.

The ready answer, though, is easy.
The pain, the beauty, the miracle...
I think I'll be hanging on
as long as I can.

# In Search of Delights

...and who can deny
they are well hidden these days?

But the heart can't get on with negatives only.
Stagnation can be worse than harm,
and I need delights,
      Now,
to prove the world hasn't lost its soul.

So, today's delight:
my black cat's vivid pink mouth
as she speaks, plaintively insisting
it is food time.
So pink. So perfect. Such a clever cat.

One delight begets another...
stay tuned.

# Relic

This old table carries a load of history.
The starry-eyed young couple
furnishing their first apartment
with Danish Modern.
Pragmatic middle-agers, agreeing that
in their new, rustic dining room,
it just didn't go.

Now, after fifty years,
it's up from the basement for another round,
suddenly back in fashion, refinished, re-loved,
re-belonging.

# Lifespan

Who are you, little one?

Where will you tuck for safekeeping
this newly hatched, still raw *you*,
still wet from birth,
years away from the dryness of age?

What need, what craving, supports the truths,
the gravitas
(avoiding world-weariness)
that allows you time to ripen?

Where to sequester
before the grand reveal,
the exercise and precision of newfound being?

# Loss of Faith

Faith goes, and what is left
is nothing special,
but what good did it do anyway?

Faith fades, then disappears, taking with it
its stock in trade:
ritual, rites of passage, belief
that something which may not be, is.

Faith lies outside the ordinary,
and so, there's no reason to pine
when it up and evaporates.
Arguably, it just got in the way, took up time,
fogged up the landscape,
inspired at best confusion, at worst derision.

Make sense?

Is it a void, or a relief,
when there's nothing left
to worship?

# Sleepless

So tired, but not asleep,
　　oh no.
I should be so lucky.
A yawn leaves me trembling with the force of it.

It's late, it's early,
almost four o'clock,
and I awoke at one.

I know, I know, the thing to do
is get up.
Read, make tea, break the cycle.
But tonight I don't obey,
I lie as one stunned,
because, who knows?
Sleep might be right on my shoulder,
ready for me.

Might, but isn't.

Tomorrow, this morning,
it won't be pretty:
low functioning, fuzzy mind...

The violence of that yawn
sends a tear trickling toward my ear
a souvenir of my miserable night.

# The Place Where You Are

I have been where you are,
the murky, muddy depths and blurred edges,
but oh, so solid.

I wish I could promise it gets easier,
that I could point you to the end game.
But I can't.

If the way is there
it will be for you only,
invisible to others,
no matter their wise words and excellent advice.

So, don't stop looking. Don't believe
this is all.
It's not.

A commitment, then, a learning
only you can undertake,
a burden only you can carry.

Trust me:
when you're ready to take the leap,
break through the muck,
it's glorious.

# The Little Things

Looking for the little things,
the unobserved things,
the secret things...

Or the ignored things,
as being too ordinary.

The way the rain puddles on the fence rail,
the birth of a bean.
Snails, gliding across the deck
for who knows what purpose.
(I rescue them, of course. They'd fry out there.)

The world has ample gaudy leaves and flowers.
Today, I engage with the subtle, the unnoticed.
The dusting of pollen,
an exploration by ants,
the changing color of the ground
as it cycles through wet and dry.

Gardens don't always behave as we want them to.
They have their own rhythms,
and horticultural skill may not suffice
to bend them to ours.

Still, all is never lost.
Through some perturbation in the laws of nature,
I have ladybugs this year.
Never mind the harvest. I watch them for hours.

# Through the Ages

I know they say we are all the ages we have lived.
In me the confused girl, unable to comprehend
something as alien as kindergarten.

Schooling, marriage, family...
Somehow, these years never knitted
into a coherent self,
one I can understand.

I feel separate,
but perhaps we all are?

Perhaps this is the reality.
Where they told us to find community,
we must know, first, the community of one.

Me.

If I ever get that part right,
maybe the rest will make sense.

# Where Does Love Go?

Where does love go
upon the death of first allure?
Is it all a matter of biology,
reproductive imperative tricked out
to look like grand emotion?
Is it prone to black holes,
sucked beyond the speed of light
with no hope of return?

Where does love go?
Nowhere, perhaps.

Is it even real? An odd obsession?
Can it be so readily transformed, like plasticine figures,
into something beyond recognition?

When it leaves, where does it go?

And does it go alone?

# Dire

Dire can't help but look like *dire*,
a word from the French
that means *say*.

*Je dis.* I say.

Do I speak dire truths?
Because, *really bad*, that's the English,
which these days, often enough, means lies,
or nothing at all, a vacuum.

(and often enough that's far too true,
but I digress.)

Two hundred years ago,
Dire got a lot more use.
But it's creeping back up.

(Funny, I would have thought, in the interim,
world wars, the cold war, and many et ceteras
might have qualified as dire.)

A dire strait is the Cape Horn of life,
tough to navigate, survival not assured.
Repeat that: Survival Not Assured.
Is that why dire is newly popular?

I would speak dire warnings,
*dire* the dire,
but why?

Why, when the sun is out
and the cats are tumbling with a new toy,
and report has come of some remarkable feat
by some remarkable grandchild,
and I just mastered a bit of Telemann?

Nope, time to retire the English
and rush to the French,
spread the good word, the positive word,
*dire, dire, dire,*
*je dis, je dis, je dis* again.

A less fraught meaning, and, mercifully, just as real.

# Survival Skills

I worry – no, I'm certain – that when the end times come
I will be found wanting, I will lack
the skills and the tools
to survive.

Take bread,
that staple since womankind
     started to bake.

Now, I bake bread,
and do it pretty well.
But in those catastrophic days
when the supply of flour runs out,
where would I get the grain?
And how would I grind it?
(Through some oversight, my kitchen lacks
one of those round stone arrangements
we see in documentaries about more 'primitive' cultures.)

And the oven...
What wood burns
at the right temperature
to bake my bread?
Once, my foremothers would have known,
but I don't.

And further, where's the wood-fired stove
to bake it in?
I had a wood stove once,
heated the whole house with it
(although I never once used it to bake bread).

But now? I'm sure
my lovely gas fireplace
won't serve.

So, in the face of cataclysm, I have
no fire, no flour, no bread –
and incidentally, no heat,
the baseboard heater as useless as the gas fireplace.
No way to warm myself
through the dark northern winter.

Ah yes, dark winter. Impossible to see my way
to the bathroom in the middle of the night
once the batteries and emergency candles
are gone – and assuming the plumbing still works.

I grow vegetables on the deck – a good survival skill,
and what do I do with them? I freeze them.
No electricity, you say? Perhaps I could dry them,
some of them,
under the pallid northern sky,
not forgetting to save the seeds.
And once the harvest's consumed?
Famine.

Friends say, you don't have
enough remaining years to worry
about such remote possibilities.
True, perhaps, but still
this sense of helplessness weighs on me,
makes me wonder
how I should now live,
what I need to learn.

# A Winter Lament

It's winter.
Early dusk erases highlights
from the chilly landscape,
flattens everything.

It has been raining for days,
water dripping from Douglas firs,
weighting down cedar boughs.
The last brown oak leaves wash to the ground
where they gather in corners.
This is a mossy, chilly world of gray skies
and little sun.

And Pat has died.

It couldn't be called unexpected.
Ninety-three years is a good span,
time enough to fill a life.

And yet... and yet...

Lawns become sodden.
The rain sends rivulets down the road.

Life belongs to memory,
transient as the rain, merging with the earth,
for Pat has died.

# A Rainy Sunday Morning in March

## Solo

Where I live, we have
an immense, private garden park.
A year's membership guarantees access.
But still,
it takes a certain defiance of norms,
and to be honest, defying myself,
to take off and go to the Park alone.

Sure, a friend would have been welcome,
on some level.

But as that wasn't to be,
why should I not enjoy the Park,
and take exactly as much time as I wish
        at some beauty spot or other,
not a moment more or less,
my actions not mediated through another's wishes?

And why should I not claim a table in the café,
enjoy my coffee and biscuit
as I watch the people,
scribbling my poems to the day
without a twinge of self-consciousness?

Why not?
(a little pep talk here...)

And so I did.

## Empty Lot

I am early, barely opening time.
In the lot, perhaps a dozen cars.

Perfect. I'll have the gardens to myself.
This morning, I plan to drink in the beauty
of the indoor display,
that greenhouse of paths
and tropical plants and fishpond.

Then, I'll wander the Park under my umbrella.

This isn't the season for full-blown glory –
    it's only March.
but oh my goodness but it's lovely, rain and all.
You feel better just for breathing the air,
so close to the ocean,
so full of every conceivable living thing.

And this morning, it's my own.

# Hyacinths

Their scent cuts through the subtle fragrance
of moist earth and tropical splendor,
through the absolute awesomeness
of the indoor garden.

I've followed the trail through this artificial jungle twice,
taken gallons, galleons, of photos.

But scent is a powerful thing
and what I remember most forcefully
is a grove of upright, dark purple hyacinths,
with their giddy aroma,
tucked in a nook by the trail.

## Greenhouses

For me, it's all about greenhouses,
the formal kind, with steamy artificial trails
wet from watering,
through tropical mass plantings.

A make-believe world, for sure,
but that's okay.

I'm early and it's raining,
no one here but me. Until
another few drift in.
They will come, look quickly, and go,
as tourists do.
But one man stops and says, "Thank you
for your great big smile."

How, I reply, could it be otherwise.
This, when outside waits in suspense
for spring to happen,
is human-made heaven, indoors.

## Tiny Souls

My thoughts turn back
to the two tiny birds,
each huddled on the pavement beside the building
housing the carousel.

Brown, they are, with darker tails,
and a hint of yellow high up on their wings.
Pine siskins, perhaps?

Did they crash into the window?
Did they make their first venture from the nest
only to find that flight is harder than it seems?

Three of us guarded them awhile,
notified the staff.

Will they be okay, these tiny beings,
bodies heaving gently, frequently, as they breathe?

I send them warmth, but I'll never know.

We want so much for nature to be perfect,
for nothing to go wrong.

If there are benevolent spirits in this garden,
I ask, bless and tend these little ones,
so helpless in the face of a fate
beyond their understanding.

# In the Coffee Shop

You know that the Park is truly deserted
when you're the only customer in the coffee shop.

For the Park's sake, I'd prefer
more visitors, a few more,
a lesson learned through Covid,
when no doubt they hung on by a thread.

Still, having the place to myself
has its allure,
as does walking under an umbrella,
a private, self-contained world,
the rain a gentle patter,
not too determined.

I'm glad to enjoy this gentle finale,
coffee, a cheese biscuit,
quiet to reflect on the gifts
of the gardens, of the day.

## Documentation

Lots of photos of flowers.
I begin to plot, as I drink my coffee...
how to recreate them on paper?

Oil pastel or pen and ink, and is it even possible
to capture their vibrancy
in black and white?

One way or another, I know
they will become something different,
however rendered.

If, that is,
my limited skill can reinvent
the barest facsimile of their glory.

## Morning's End

I can only sit still for so long, it seems,
before I itch to be on the move.

My cheese biscuit is a quarter uneaten,
coffee still a weight in the lidded cup
    (compostable)
yet now, I'm thinking of home.

Ready to get back to the overwhelmingly familiar –
as opposed to my nodding acquaintance
with this miraculous park.

But, no. I refuse to give up my morning out
quite so easily.

Relax, woman!
Enjoy the feasts you've experienced
on this damp gray day.
A sampling of bliss can go a long way,
and each breath of gratitude
    helps to create
    a world so desperately in need
    of beauty.

## Home Again

Welcoming me home, my cat purrs and purrs.
An indoor cat, she is unaware
life could be less comfortable, require more daring.
Hers is a world of warmth,
soft beds,
the imminent promise of food.

Her perspective is different from mine this morning,
but equally valuable, equally satisfying
to the heart.

## About The Author

Elizabeth Carson lives and writes in Victoria, British Columbia, Canada.

To learn more about her life and work, please visit lizanncarson.com.

www.ingramcontent.com/pod-product-compliance
Lightning Source LLC
Chambersburg PA
CBHW071504070426
42452CB00041B/2295